# ·My·First·
# Atlas

First published in Great Britain in 1991 by
World International Publishing Ltd.,
in association with Joshua Morris Publishing Inc.
First reprint 1992.
All rights reserved.
World International Publishing Ltd.,
an Egmont Company, Egmont House,
P.O. Box 111, Great Ducie Street, Manchester M60 3BL.
Copyright © 1991 Joshua Morris Publishing, Inc. and Alan Snow.
Illustrations © 1991 Alan Snow.
Text by Times Four Publishing Ltd.
Printed in Italy.
No part of this book may be reproduced
without written permission from the copyright owner.

**British Library Cataloguing in Publication Data**
Snow, Alan
My first atlas.
1. Atlases
I. Title
912

# ·My ·First·
# Atlas

## Illustrated by
## Alan
## Snow

World International Publishing Limited
Manchester

# North America

Canada, the United States of America, Mexico and the Caribbean region are all part of North America.

The NASA Space Centre is in Florida, USA.

New York is the biggest city in the USA.

**US flag**

The **USA** is divided into 50 states, including Alaska and the Pacific islands of Hawaii. It is one of the world's richest countries. It has supplies of oil and gas, and it has lots of factories and good farmland.

The USA grows more **wheat** than any other country.

## STATE KEY

| | | |
|---|---|---|
| 1 Alabama | 19 Maine | 35 Ohio |
| 2 Alaska | 20 Maryland | 36 Oklahoma |
| 3 Arizona | 21 Massachusetts | 37 Oregon |
| 4 Arkansas | 22 Michigan | 38 Pennsylvania |
| 5 California | 23 Minnesota | 39 Rhode Island |
| 6 Colorado | 24 Mississippi | 40 South |
| 7 Connecticut | 25 Missouri | Carolina |
| 8 Delaware | 26 Montana | 41 South Dakota |
| 9 Florida | 27 Nebraska | 42 Tennessee |
| 10 Georgia | 28 Nevada | 43 Texas |
| 11 Hawaii | 29 New | 44 Utah |
| 12 Idaho | Hampshire | 45 Vermont |
| 13 Illinois | 30 New Jersey | 46 Virginia |
| 14 Indiana | 31 New Mexico | 47 Washington |
| 15 Iowa | 32 New York | 48 West Virginia |
| 16 Kansas | 33 North | 49 Wisconsin |
| 17 Kentucky | Carolina | 50 Wyoming |
| 18 Louisiana | 34 North Dakota | |

**Baffin Island**

**Hudson Bay**

**CANADA**

Vancouver

**Pacific Ocean**

San Francisco

Los Angeles

**USA**

Dallas

New Orleans

**MEXICO**

Mexico City

Chica[go]

**Mexican flag**

There are hot, dry deserts in the north of **Mexico**. Farther south are rain forests.

Desert  Semi-Desert  Tundra  Evergreen Forest

Grassland  Broadleaf Forest  Tropical Forest  Mountains

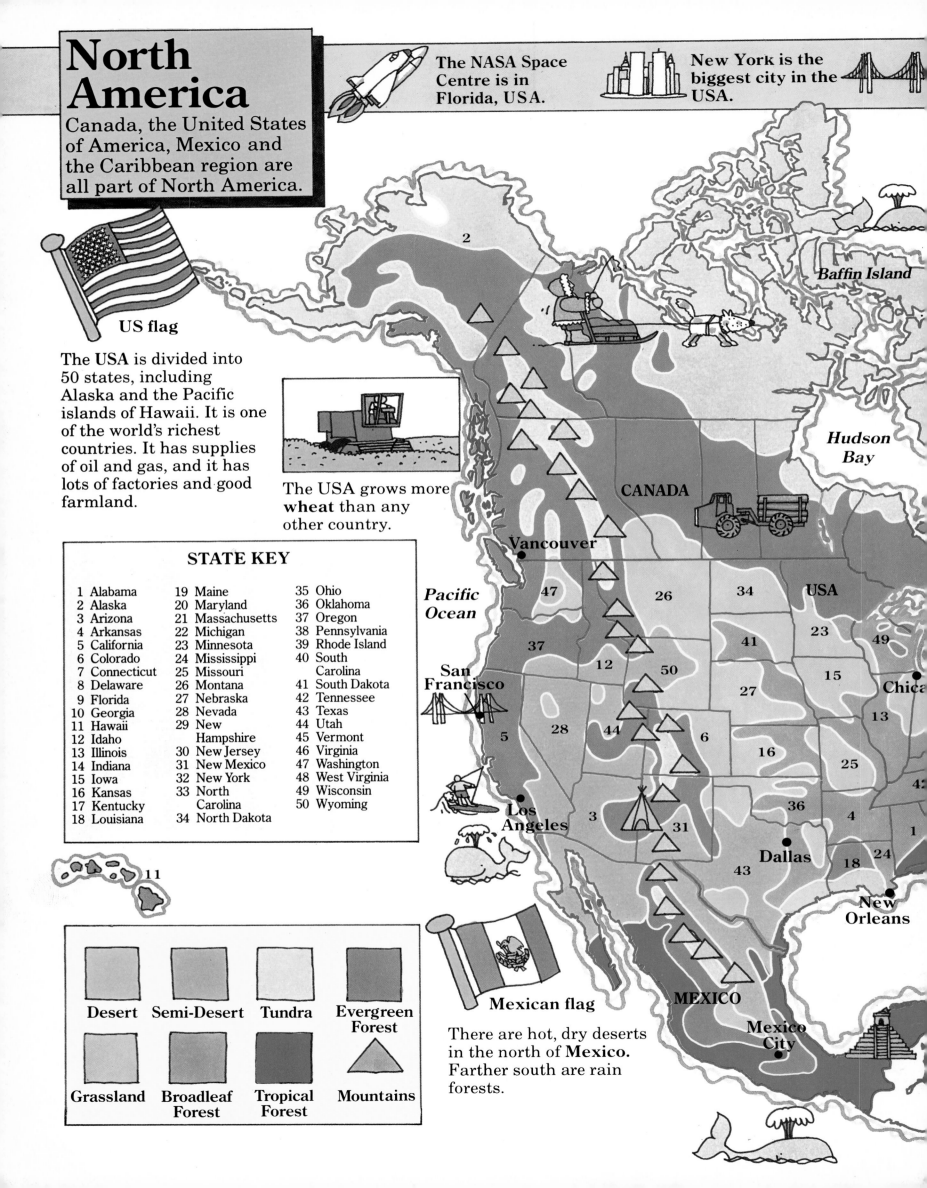

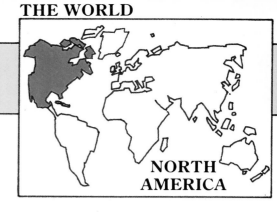

The famous Golden
Gate Bridge is
San Francisco.

The ancient Maya
once built cities in
Mexico.

High mountains run all the way down the west coast. They
stretch from Alaska in the north to Mexico in the south. In
Canada and the USA, they are known as the **Rocky
Mountains**. In Mexico, they are known as the **Sierra Madres**.

Canadian flag

**Canada** is the world's second largest
country in area. In the north it has
many lakes and forests where such
animals as elk, moose, deer and
wolves live. In the south it has huge
flat lands where farmers grow wheat
and other crops.

Most Canadians live in the warmer
southern parts of the country, where
there are some big cities. In the far
north, ice and snow cover the ground
for most of the year.

Canadian mountain scenery

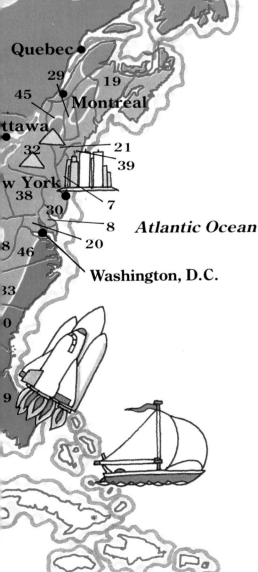

Quebec

29        19
45
     Montreal
ttawa
  32        21
              39
w York
38
    30
          8      *Atlantic Ocean*
     20
8  46
        Washington, D.C.
33

0

9

*Caribbean Sea*

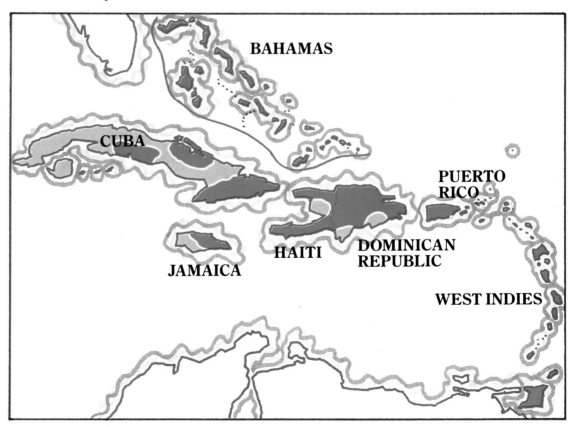

BAHAMAS

CUBA

PUERTO
RICO

HAITI    DOMINICAN
         REPUBLIC

JAMAICA

WEST INDIES

The Caribbean Sea is an arm of the Atlantic Ocean off the coast of
mainland North America. Cuba and the West Indies are here, along
with many smaller islands. The climate is very warm, and the area is
a popular place for tourists to visit. The hot weather is good for
growing sugar cane and bananas. However, sometimes hurricanes
sweep over the land and cause lots of damage.

# Central and South America

The continent of South America is about 4,500 miles (7,241 kilometres) long. It has deserts, rain forests, mountains, and grasslands. Central America is the thin piece of land that joins Mexico to South America.

High in the Andes sits ancient Machu Picchu city.

Fierce piranha fish live in the Amazon River.

## CENTRAL AMERICA

BELIZE

GUATEMALA

HONDURAS

EL SALVADOR

NICARAGUA

COSTA RICA

PANAMA

Panama Canal

Panama City

High mountains, called the **Andes,** run all the way down the west coast of South America. Many of the Andean mountain people keep animals called **llamas.** They can carry heavy loads over slippery or rocky ground. Llamas also give people meat, wool and milk.

FRENCH GUIANA

SURINAM

GUYANA

Caracas

VENEZUELA

Bogota

COLOMBIA

Quito

ECUADOR

PERU

*Amazon River*

*Amazon Jungle*

BRAZIL

Lima

Machu Picchu

BOLIVIA

La Paz

*Pacific Ocean*

*Andes*

*Atacama Desert*

Santiago

CHILE

ARGENTINA

### Legend

| Mountains | Bananas | Cocoa | Coffee | Industrial Area | Llamas | Sheep | Cattle |
|---|---|---|---|---|---|---|---|

| Desert | Scrub | Grassland | Evergreen Forest | Thorn Forest | Temperate Forest | Rain Forest | Alpine |
|---|---|---|---|---|---|---|---|

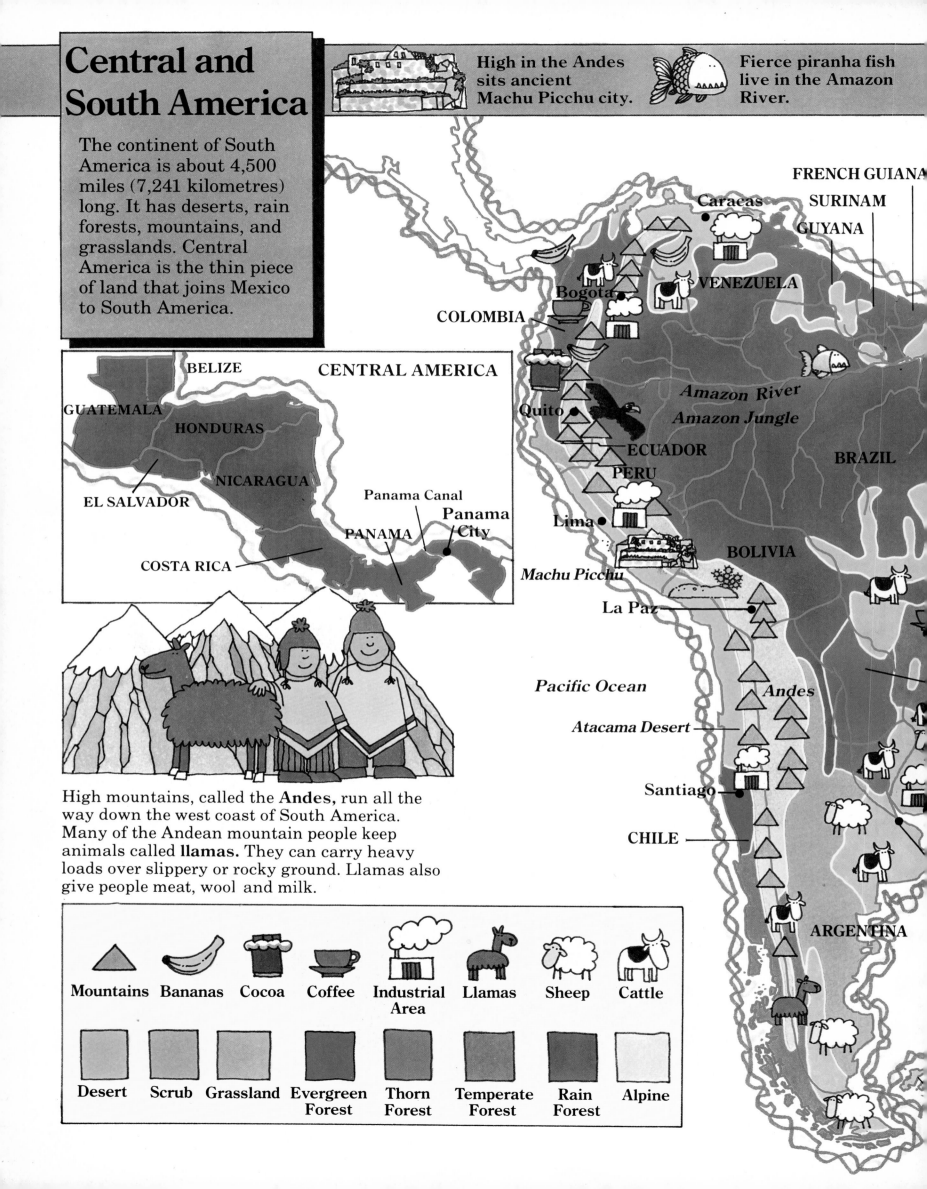

The first **South American people** were American Indians. Then people from Spain, Portugal and Africa came to live there. Many of the people living there today are a mixture of races.

**Early American Indian objects**

*Atlantic Ocean*

There are still some **Indian tribes** living in the South American jungles. They survive by hunting animals and eating jungle plants.

**Brazilian flag**

More than half of Brazil is covered by hot steamy jungle called rain forest. It grows around the **Amazon,** which is one of the biggest rivers in the world. The Amazon begins in the Andes mountains and flows all the way across Brazil to the Atlantic Ocean. Large boats can sail only part of the way up the river. After that, the best way to travel is by smaller boats such as canoes.

asilia

Rio de Janeiro

PARAGUAY

URUGUAY

ontevideo

enos Aires

Lots of **animals and plants** live in the rain forest. But their home is threatened because large parts of the forest are being chopped down. Many people are trying to stop this from happening because the forests are important to everybody in the world. The trees help to clean the air and make it better for everyone to breathe. Here are some rain forest animals:

Macaw

Hummingbird

Howler monkey

Jaguar

Toucan

Sloth

Caiman

kland Islands

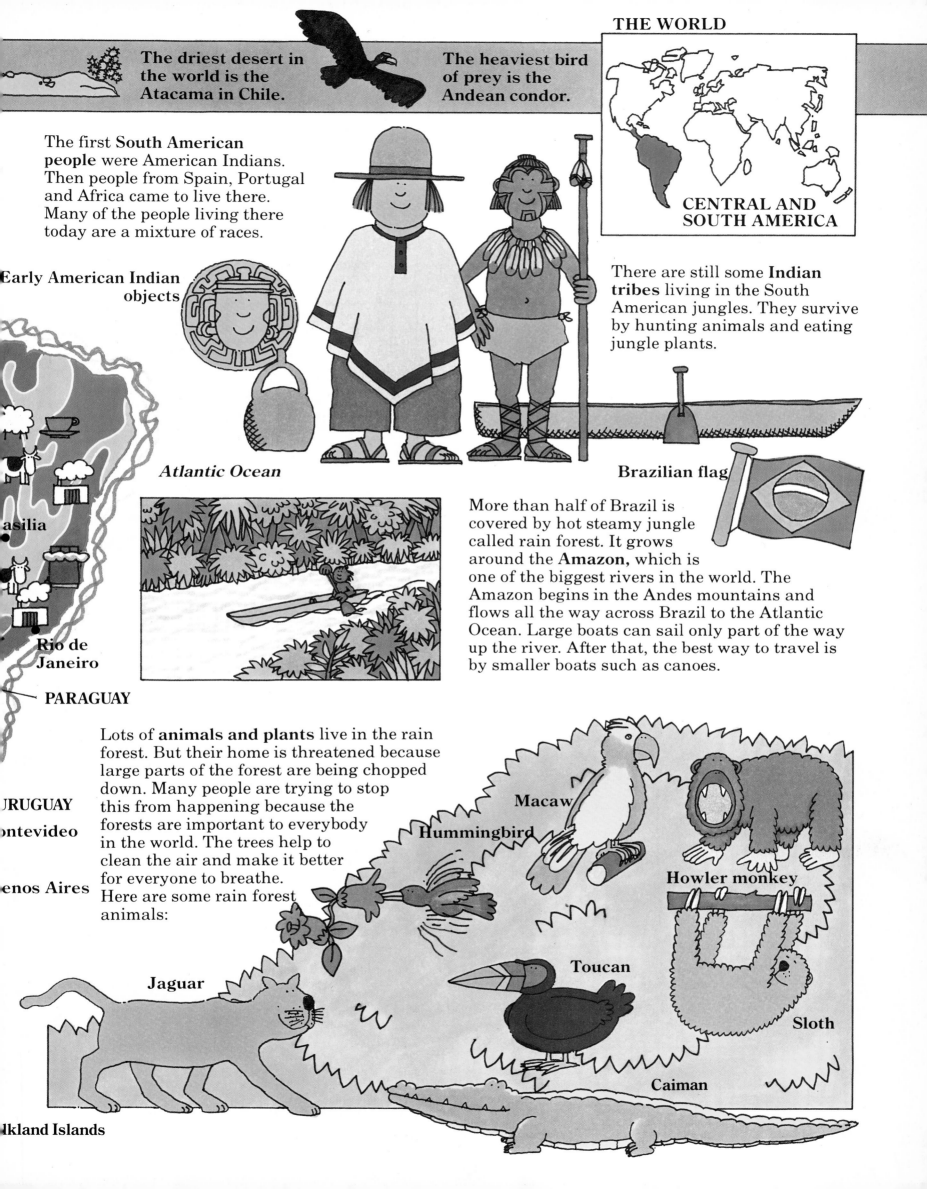

# Northern Europe

Europe stretches from the cold Arctic Ocean in the north to the hot lands around the Mediterranean. This map shows the northern part of Europe. The area in the far north is called Scandinavia.

In the far north are herds of reindeer.

One of London's most famous sights is the Tower of Lond[on]

**Scandinavia** includes Norway, Sweden, Denmark, Finland, and Iceland. In the far north the sun shines all through the night in summer, but not at all in winter.

Ar[ctic]

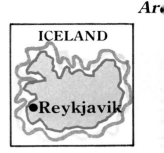

ICELAND

•Reykjavik

**British flag**

**The United Kingdom** is made up of Scotland, Wales, England, and Northern Ireland. The capital city is London.

**Fishing** is important around the coastline of northern Europe.

There are many **factories** in northern Europe. Some of them are used for making machinery such as cars, trucks, and TVs. There are coal mines and steel-making plants, too.

In **the Republic of Ireland** the land is mainly used for farming. There is plenty of good fishing around the coasts.

NORWAY

UNITED KINGDOM

*Atlantic Ocean*

*North Sea*

*SCOTLAND*

Glasgow

Edinburgh

DENMA[RK]

*NORTHERN IRELAND*

*REPUBLIC OF IRELAND*

Belfast

Dublin

Hambur[g]

*ENGLAND*

*WALES*

*Rhine River*

London

Bonn

Frankfur[t]

GERMANY

LIECHTENSTEIN

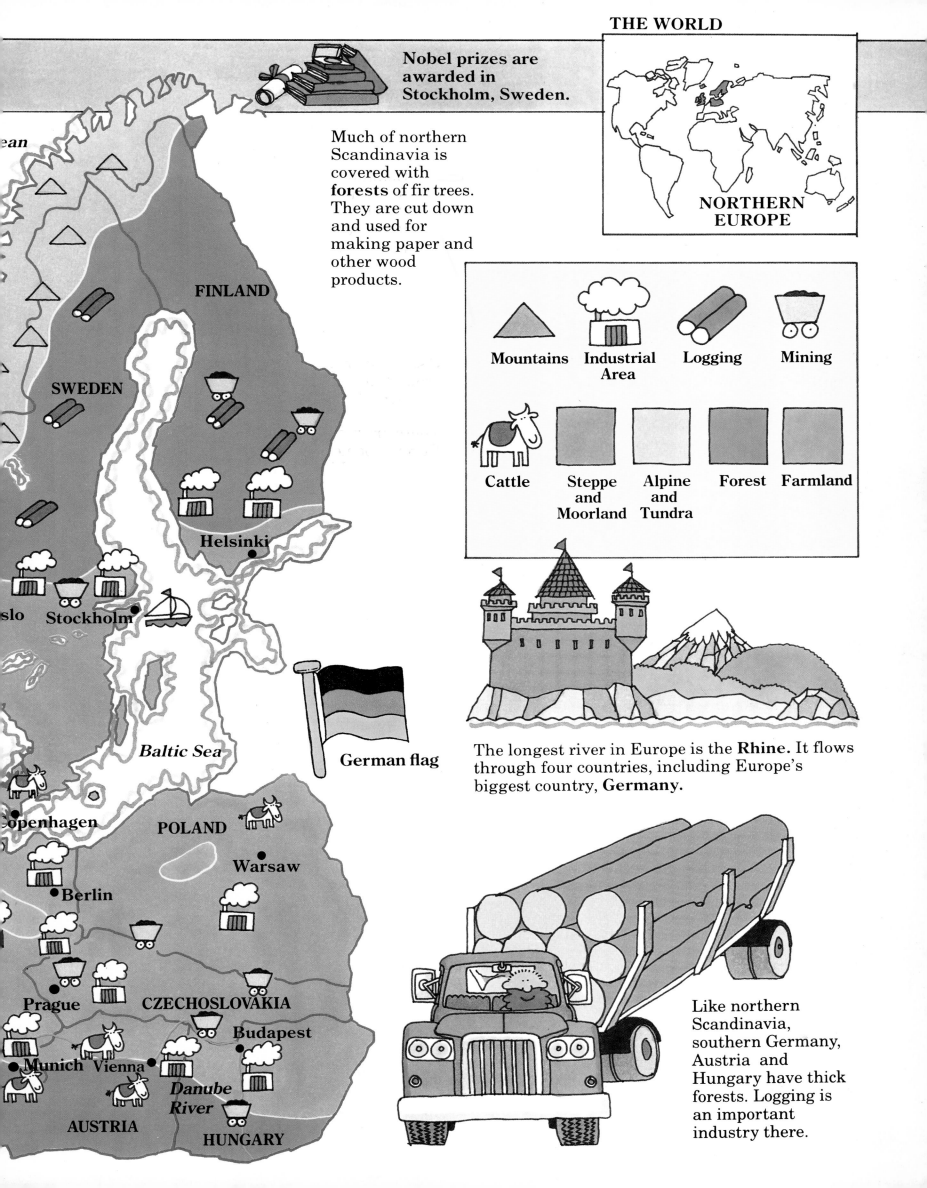

Nobel prizes are awarded in Stockholm, Sweden.

Much of northern Scandinavia is covered with **forests** of fir trees. They are cut down and used for making paper and other wood products.

FINLAND

SWEDEN

Helsinki

Mountains    Industrial Area    Logging    Mining

Cattle    Steppe and Moorland    Alpine and Tundra    Forest    Farmland

Oslo

Stockholm

Baltic Sea

**German flag**

The longest river in Europe is the **Rhine.** It flows through four countries, including Europe's biggest country, **Germany.**

Copenhagen

POLAND

Warsaw

Berlin

CZECHOSLOVAKIA

Prague

Budapest

Munich    Vienna

*Danube River*

AUSTRIA    HUNGARY

Like northern Scandinavia, southern Germany, Austria and Hungary have thick forests. Logging is an important industry there.

# Southern Europe

The countries in southern parts of Europe are hot and sunny in summertime. The southern coastline is beside the warm Mediterranean Sea. It has lots of popular summer holiday resorts.

The **Eiffel Tower** is in Paris, the capital of France.

Buildings from 400 B.C. still stand Greece's Acropolis

The **Netherlands** is a very flat country. Much of the land was once covered by sea, but Dutch engineers have drained away the water and built dams called **dikes** to keep it out. The drained areas of land are called **polders.**

**NETHERLANDS**

Amsterdam

Rotterdam

Brussels
BELGIUM

French flag

Paris          LUXEMBOURG

Atlantic Ocean

FRANCE

The countries around the Mediterranean have a warm climate that is good for **farming.** Many farmers in Spain, France and Italy grow grapes and olives. The warm weather is also good for growing fruit such as oranges and lemons.

Bay of Biscay

Lyon

Mc
Bla

ANDORR

**Swiss flag**

In Switzerland there are high mountains called the **Alps.** They are popular for skiing.

Madrid

PORTUGAL

SPAIN

Majorca

**Spanish flag**

Lisbon

More tourists visit **Spain** than any other European country. It has lots of sandy beaches.

Gibraltar

AFRICA

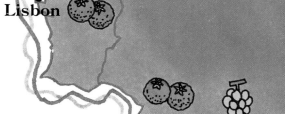

Venice, Italy, has canals through it instead of roads.

Mont Blanc in France is the highest point in the Alps.

About two thousand years ago the **Romans** conquered southern Europe. You can still see the remains of their cities. They built Rome, capital of Italy.

THE WORLD

SOUTHERN EUROPE

SWITZERLAND

Zurich

ne

Geneva

Venice

ONACO

Corsica

Sardinia

Mediterranean Sea

SLOVENIA

CROATIA

BOSNIA AND HERCEGOVINA

*SERBIA*

Belgrade

YUGOSLAVIA

*MONTENEGRO*

*MACEDONIA*

Tirana

ALBANIA

ROMANIA

Bucharest

Danube River

Sofia

BULGARIA

Black Sea

Istanbul

TURKEY

*Aegean Sea*

Rome

ITALY

*Adriatic Sea*

GREECE

Athens

Sicily

Crete

**Legend:**

| Industrial Area | Citrus Fruit | Holiday Resort | Grapes | Mountains | Skiing | Apples |

| Alpine | Coniferous Forest | Evergreen Forest | Broadleaf Forest | Grassland | Steppe and Semi-Desert |

# Africa

Africa is a huge continent divided into many countries. There are deserts in the north and south, where very little rain falls. In the middle are jungles.

Timbuktu is a city of mud huts in Mali.

Mt. Kilimanjaro is Africa's highest poi...

The **Sahara Desert,** in North Africa, is the largest desert in the world. During the day it is very hot, but at night it is cold. The Saharan people use camels for travel over the sand. The camels can go for days without water.

Algiers

Casablanca

MOROCCO

WESTERN SAHARA

ALGERIA

TUNISIA

MAURITANIA

MALI

Timbuktu

NIGE...

SENEGAL

GAMBIA

*Niger River*

GUINEA-BISSAU

GUINEA

BURKINA FASO

BENIN

NIGERIA

SIERRA LEONE

LIBERIA

IVORY COAST

GHANA

TOGO

Lagos

CAMERO...

GABON

There are some large African cities, but most people live in small villages where they farm land and look after their cattle. They often live in groups called **tribes.**

EQUATORIAL GUINEA

*Atlantic Ocean*

There are wide grassy plains called **grasslands** in Africa. Herds of wild animals wander over the grasslands in search of food. Zebras, elephants and giraffes eat the leaves of the trees and bushes. Lions and cheetahs hunt the plant-eating animals.

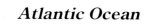

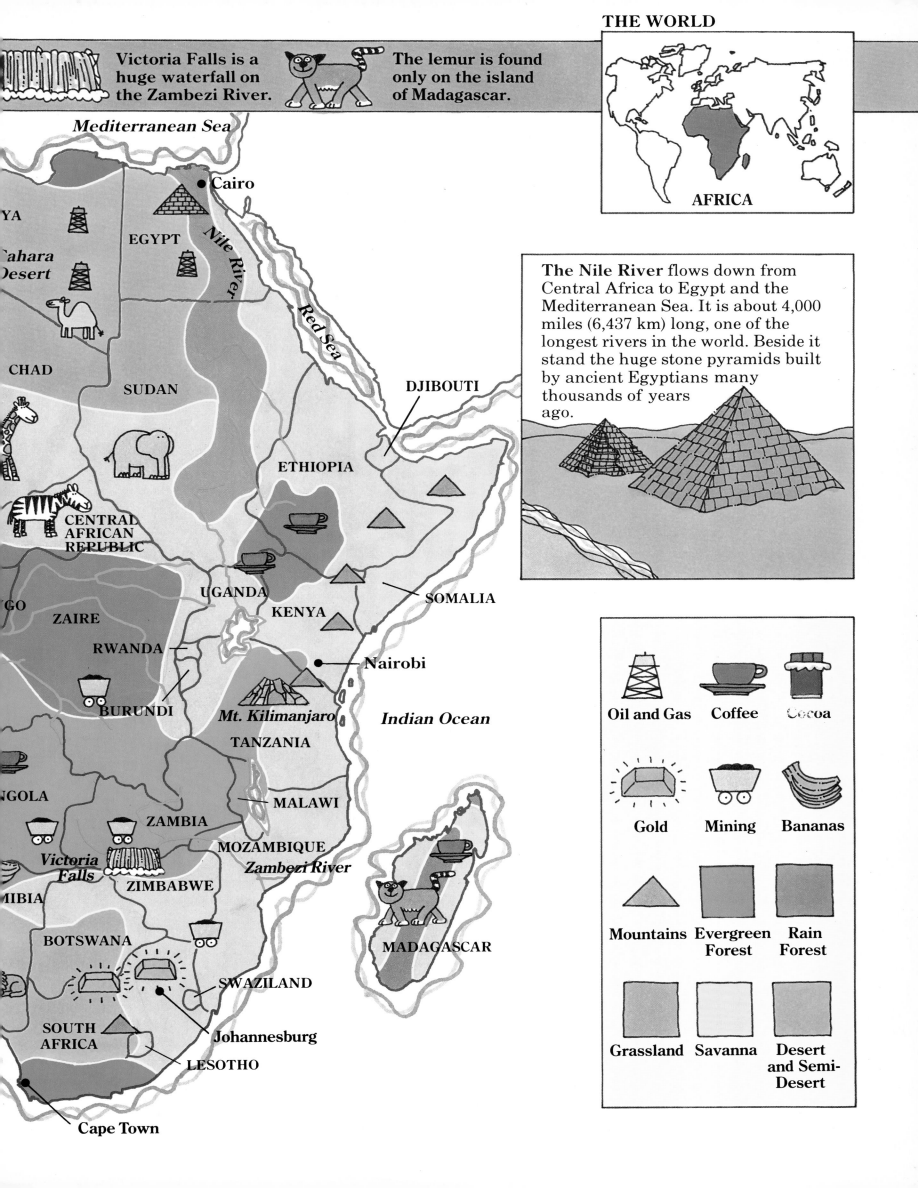

Victoria Falls is a huge waterfall on the Zambezi River.

The lemur is found only on the island of Madagascar.

**THE WORLD**

AFRICA

Mediterranean Sea

Cairo

EGYPT

YA

Sahara Desert

CHAD

SUDAN

Nile River

Red Sea

DJIBOUTI

ETHIOPIA

**The Nile River** flows down from Central Africa to Egypt and the Mediterranean Sea. It is about 4,000 miles (6,437 km) long, one of the longest rivers in the world. Beside it stand the huge stone pyramids built by ancient Egyptians many thousands of years ago.

CENTRAL AFRICAN REPUBLIC

UGANDA

GO

ZAIRE

KENYA

SOMALIA

RWANDA

BURUNDI

Nairobi

Mt. Kilimanjaro

Indian Ocean

TANZANIA

GOLA

MALAWI

ZAMBIA

MOZAMBIQUE

Zambezi River

Victoria Falls

ZIMBABWE

MIBIA

MADAGASCAR

Oil and Gas    Coffee    Cocoa

Gold    Mining    Bananas

Mountains    Evergreen Forest    Rain Forest

BOTSWANA

SWAZILAND

SOUTH AFRICA

Johannesburg

LESOTHO

Cape Town

Grassland    Savanna    Desert and Semi-Desert

# CIS

The USSR (the Soviet Union), born in the Russian Revolution of 1917, came to an end in 1991. In its place stands the CIS (Commonwealth of Independent States).

The deepest lake in the world is Lake Baikal.

Many churches in the CIS have round domes.

About a third of the land occupied by the CIS is covered in **forests.** Elk, deer, and bears are some of the animals found there.

In some areas the trees are cut into logs to make wooden products and paper.

**Russia** is the largest of the CIS countries. It has an area over six times greater than the next largest, Kazakhstan. Russia's population is nearly three times larger than the next most crowded CIS country, Ukraine.

Estonia, Latvia, Lithuania and Georgia are not in the CIS, but they were in the USSR. A small part of Russia lies between Lithuania and Poland.

The CIS countries have many different kinds of people and over 100 languages.

**Deserts,** where few plants grow and very few people live, make up a large portion of the area in the southern CIS.

Between the forests and the deserts are vast, flat, grassy plains called **steppes.** This land is good for growing wheat and other crops.

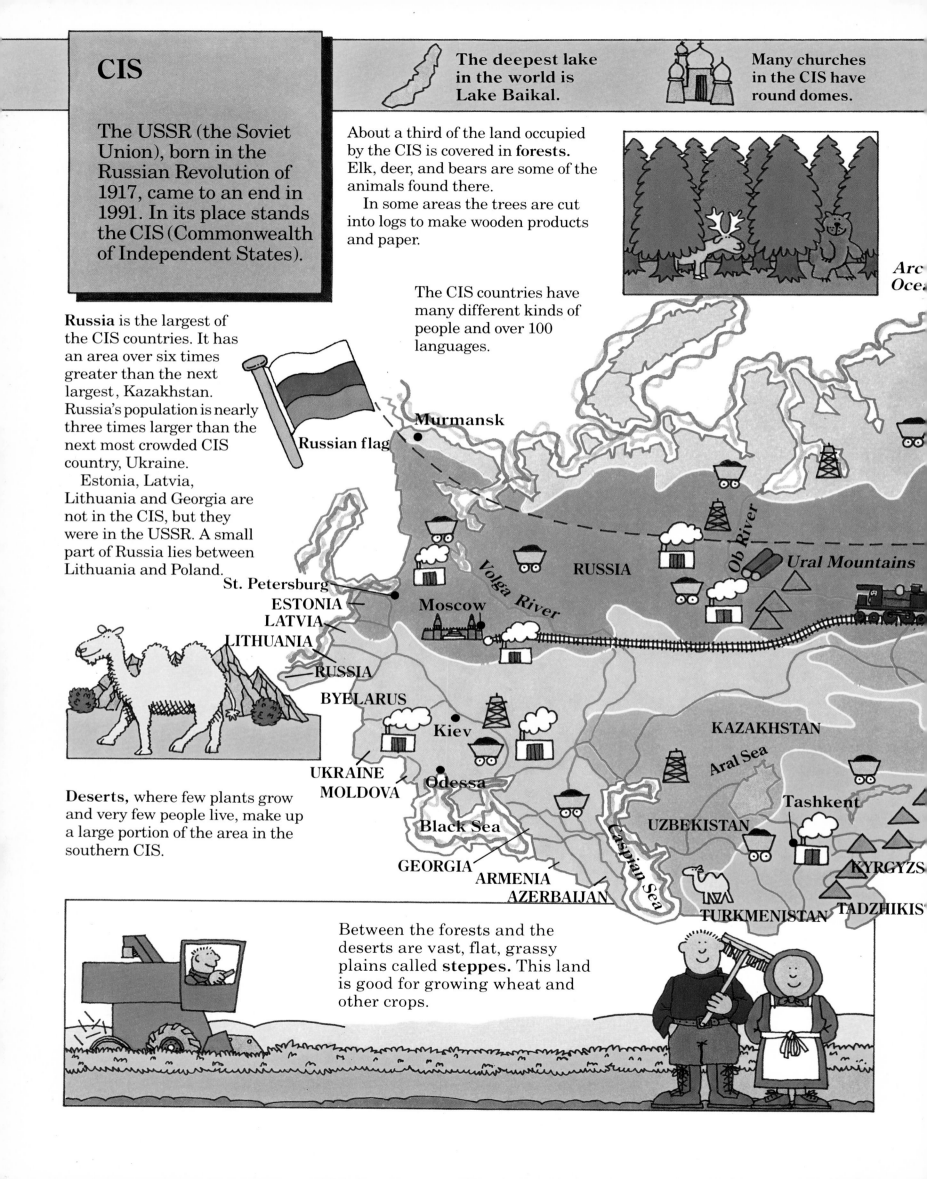

Arc Oce.

Russian flag

Murmansk

St. Petersburg
ESTONIA
LATVIA
LITHUANIA
RUSSIA
BYELARUS
UKRAINE
MOLDOVA

Moscow

Volga River

RUSSIA

Ob River

Ural Mountains

Kiev

Odessa

Black Sea

GEORGIA
ARMENIA
AZERBAIJAN

Caspian Sea

Aral Sea

KAZAKHSTAN

UZBEKISTAN

Tashkent

KYRGYZS

TURKMENISTAN TADZHIKIS

 The Kremlin in Moscow houses a famous museum.

 The Trans-Siberian Railway is the longest in the world.

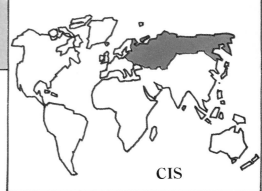

CIS

In the north of Russia are huge areas where it is so cold that the ground is frozen for most of the year. These parts are called **tundra.** Herds of reindeer live there.

The northeast part of the area called **Siberia** is famous for its freezing winters.

Part of Russia is inside the **Arctic Circle,** an imaginary line drawn on maps around the North Pole. Inside the circle it is always very cold.

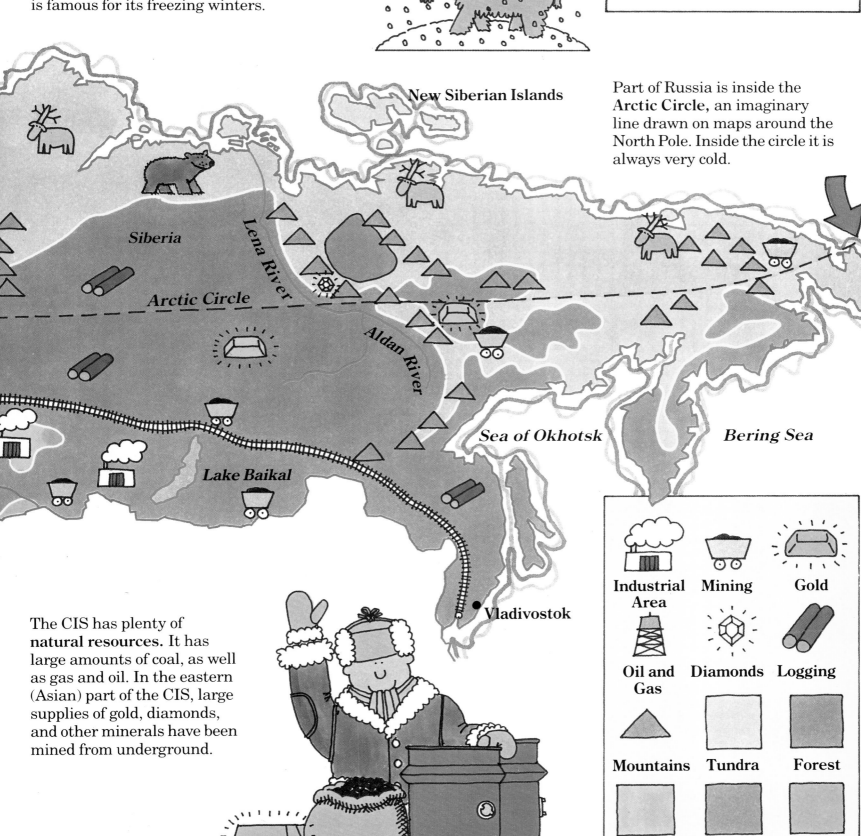

New Siberian Islands

*Siberia*

*Lena River*

*Arctic Circle*

*Aldan River*

*Sea of Okhotsk*

*Bering Sea*

*Lake Baikal*

● Vladivostok

The CIS has plenty of **natural resources.** It has large amounts of coal, as well as gas and oil. In the eastern (Asian) part of the CIS, large supplies of gold, diamonds, and other minerals have been mined from underground.

**Industrial Area**   **Mining**   **Gold**

**Oil and Gas**   **Diamonds**   **Logging**

**Mountains**   **Tundra**   **Forest**

**Farmland**   **Steppe and Semi-Desert**   **Desert**

# Asia

Asia is a huge continent stretching from the Mediterranean Sea to the Pacific Ocean. More than half the world's people live there. This map shows the Middle East and southern Asia.

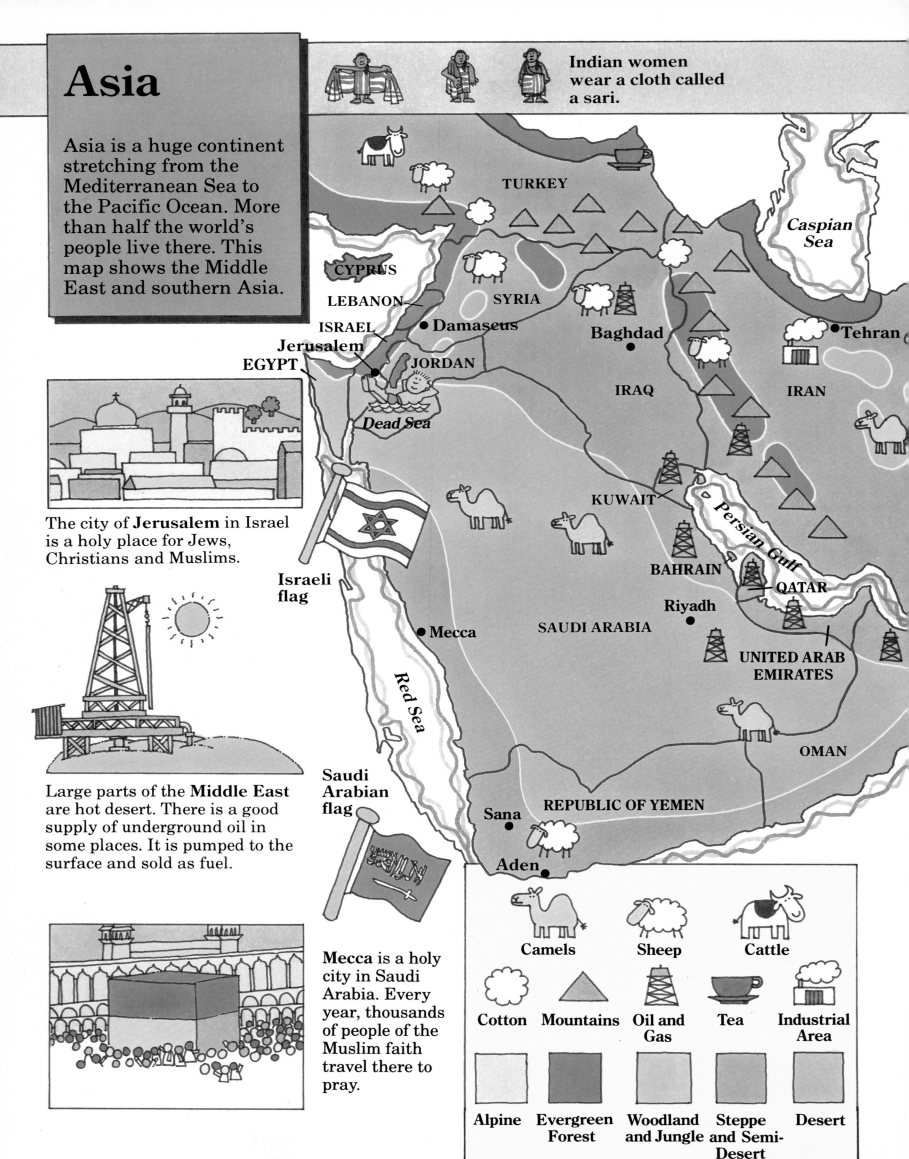

Indian women wear a cloth called a sari.

The city of **Jerusalem** in Israel is a holy place for Jews, Christians and Muslims.

Large parts of the **Middle East** are hot desert. There is a good supply of underground oil in some places. It is pumped to the surface and sold as fuel.

Israeli flag

Saudi Arabian flag

**Mecca** is a holy city in Saudi Arabia. Every year, thousands of people of the Muslim faith travel there to pray.

TURKEY

Caspian Sea

CYPRUS

LEBANON

ISRAEL

Jerusalem

EGYPT

JORDAN

Dead Sea

Damascus

Baghdad

SYRIA

Tehran

IRAQ

IRAN

KUWAIT

Persian Gulf

BAHRAIN

QATAR

Riyadh

SAUDI ARABIA

UNITED ARAB EMIRATES

Mecca

Red Sea

OMAN

REPUBLIC OF YEMEN

Sana

Aden

Camels    Sheep    Cattle

Cotton    Mountains    Oil and Gas    Tea    Industrial Area

Alpine    Evergreen Forest    Woodland and Jungle    Steppe and Semi-Desert    Desert

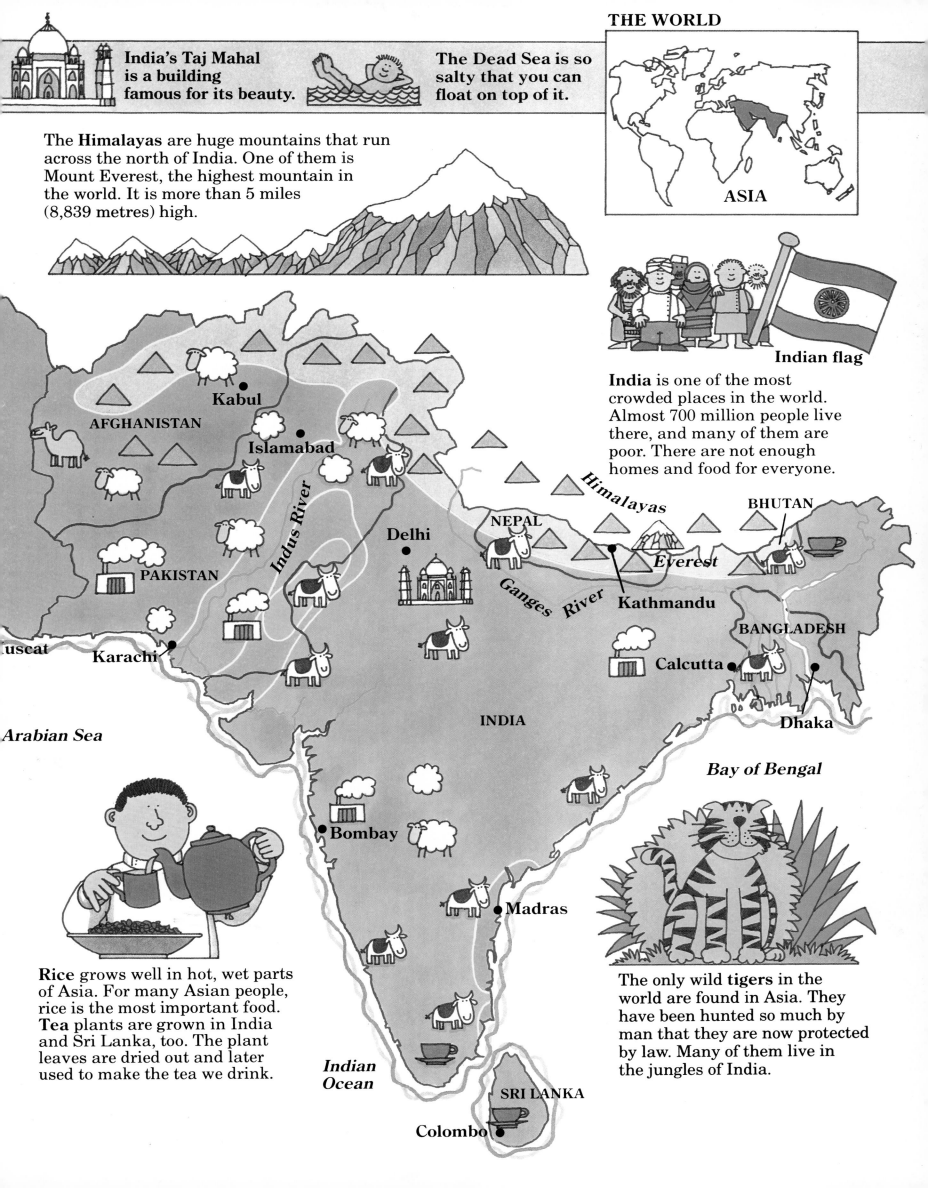

India's **Taj Mahal** is a building famous for its beauty.

The **Dead Sea** is so salty that you can float on top of it.

THE WORLD

ASIA

The **Himalayas** are huge mountains that run across the north of India. One of them is Mount Everest, the highest mountain in the world. It is more than 5 miles (8,839 metres) high.

**Indian flag**

**India** is one of the most crowded places in the world. Almost 700 million people live there, and many of them are poor. There are not enough homes and food for everyone.

AFGHANISTAN

Kabul

Islamabad

PAKISTAN

Indus River

Delhi

NEPAL

Himalayas

BHUTAN

Everest

Ganges River

Kathmandu

Karachi

uscat

BANGLADESH

Calcutta

Dhaka

Arabian Sea

INDIA

Bay of Bengal

Bombay

Madras

**Rice** grows well in hot, wet parts of Asia. For many Asian people, rice is the most important food. **Tea** plants are grown in India and Sri Lanka, too. The plant leaves are dried out and later used to make the tea we drink.

The only wild **tigers** in the world are found in Asia. They have been hunted so much by man that they are now protected by law. Many of them live in the jungles of India.

Indian Ocean

SRI LANKA

Colombo

# Far East

China's capital is the ancient city of Beijing.

This map shows the rest of Asia, including China and Japan. There are many islands in the ocean around this part of Asia. It is sometimes called the Far East.

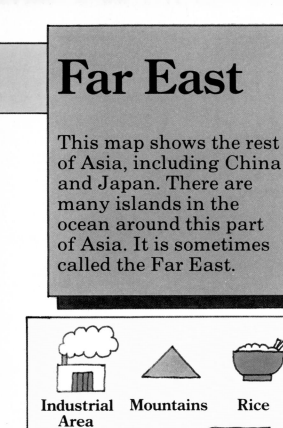

**Industrial Area** | **Mountains** | **Rice** | **Tea** | **Sheep**

**Cotton** | **Rubber** | **Desert** | **Scrub and Semi-Desert** | **Alpine**

**Coniferous Forest** | **Grassland** | **Broadleaf Forest** | **Temperate Rain Forest** | **Tropical Rain Forest**

MONGOLIA

Great Wall

CHINA

Himalayas

Tibet

Lhasa

Chinese flag

Kunming

MYANMAR

LAOS

Han

THAILAND

Bangkok

*Indian Ocean*

KAMPUCHEA

Phnom Penh

VIETNAM

Kuala Lumpur

Sumatra

Singapo

Jakarta

**China** has more people living in it than any other country. Over one billion people, about a fifth of all the people in the world, live there.

An enormous stone wall stretches for about 4,000 miles (6,400 kilometres) across part of China. It is called the **Great Wall of China**, and it is so big that astronauts can see it from space! It was built long ago to keep enemies out of the country. Nowadays you can visit parts of it.

Not many Chinese people have cars, but many have **bicycles**. There are about 210 million bicycles in China! If you visited a Chinese city, you would see streets crowded with people on bicycles.

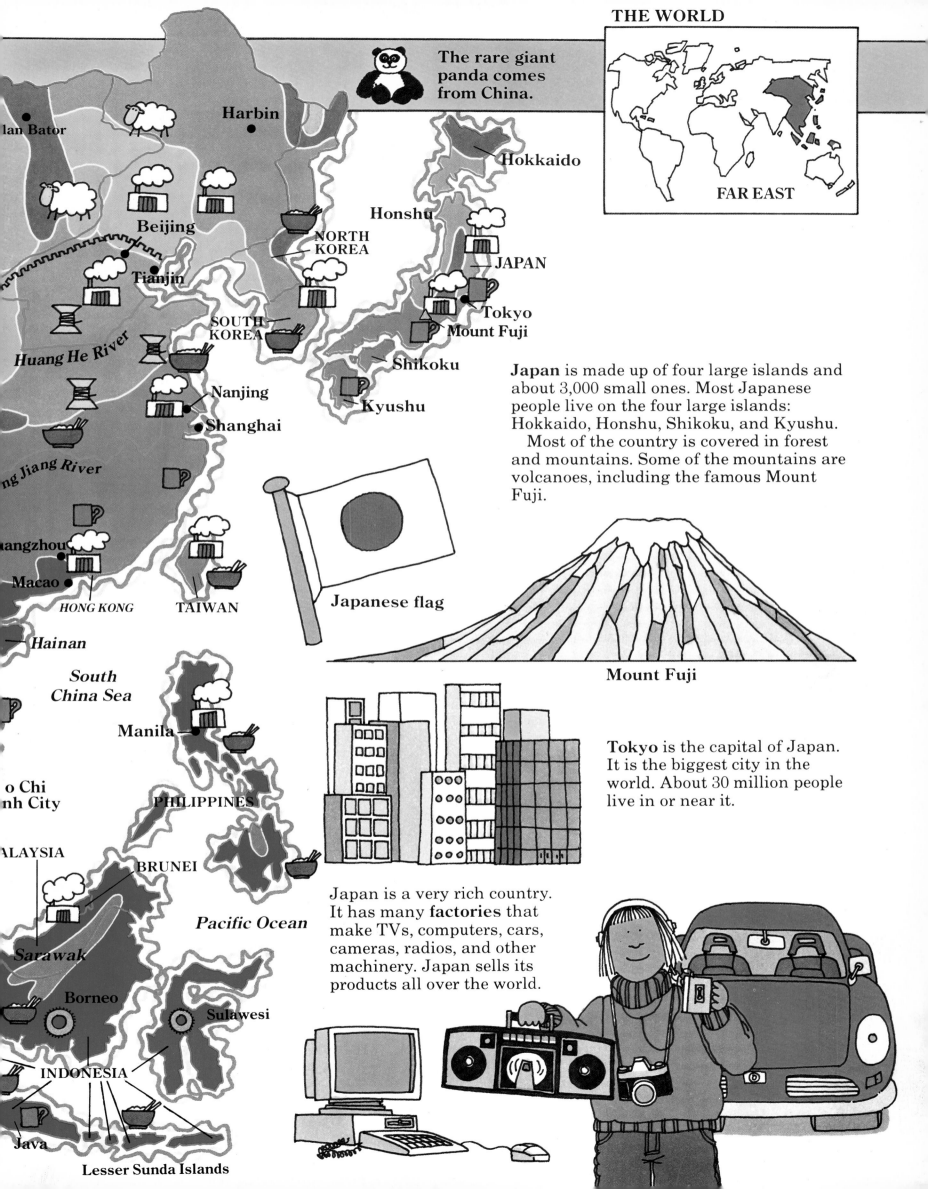

The rare giant panda comes from China.

Harbin

Hokkaido

Honshu

ۚlan Bator

Beijing

NORTH KOREA

JAPAN

Tianjin

Huang He River

SOUTH KOREA

Tokyo
Mount Fuji

Shikoku

Nanjing

Kyushu

Shanghai

ᵍ Jiang River

Japanese flag

**Japan** is made up of four large islands and about 3,000 small ones. Most Japanese people live on the four large islands: Hokkaido, Honshu, Shikoku, and Kyushu.

Most of the country is covered in forest and mountains. Some of the mountains are volcanoes, including the famous Mount Fuji.

ᵘangzhou

Macao

HONG KONG

TAIWAN

Hainan

South China Sea

Manila

**Tokyo** is the capital of Japan. It is the biggest city in the world. About 30 million people live in or near it.

Mount Fuji

ᵒ Chi
ᵑh City

PHILIPPINES

Japan is a very rich country. It has many **factories** that make TVs, computers, cars, cameras, radios, and other machinery. Japan sells its products all over the world.

ᴬLAYSIA

BRUNEI

Pacific Ocean

Sarawak

Borneo

Sulawesi

INDONESIA

Java

Lesser Sunda Islands

# Australia and New Zealand

Australia is the smallest continent. About four fifths of it is covered in desert. New Zealand is made up of two large islands and several small ones. New Guinea is the world's second largest island.

Ayers Rock is the largest block of stone in the world.

Australia has a coral reef called th Great Barrier Reef

There are many large **sheep farms** in Australia. The sheep provide people with meat and wool.

The first people to live in Australia were **aborigines.** They gathered nuts and berries and hunted animals for food. There are still some aborigine tribes living in parts of Australia.

*Indian Ocean*

Darwin

*Northern Territ*

*Western Australia*

**AUSTRALIA**

Australia has some unusual animals that are not found anywhere else in the world. Here are some examples:

**Kangaroos** carry their babies in pouches.

Furry **koalas** live in trees.

**Australian flag**

Perth

*Great Australian Big*

The **duck-billed platypus** has fur and a beak like a duck.

The east coast of Australia has the most rainfall. Many of the **cities** are there.

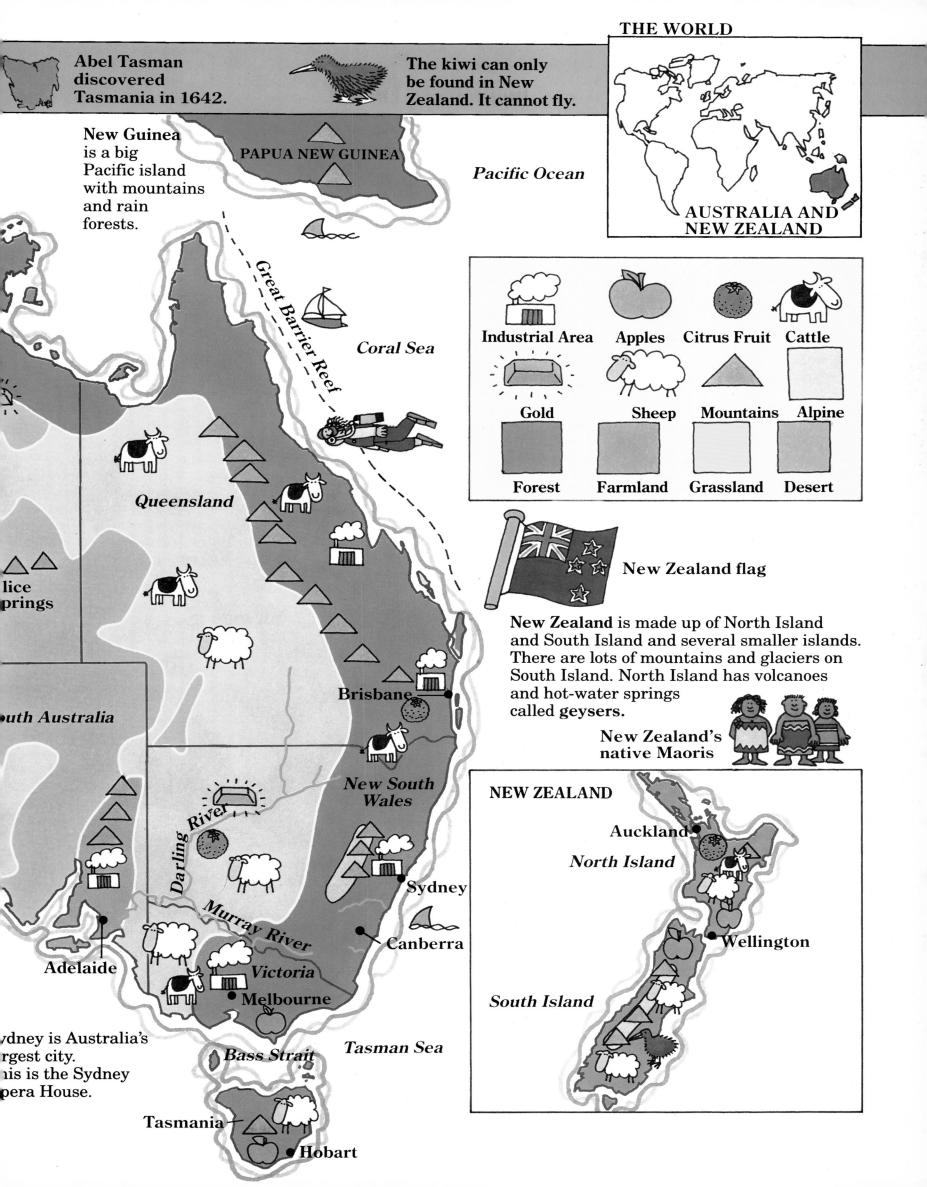

Abel Tasman discovered Tasmania in 1642.

The kiwi can only be found in New Zealand. It cannot fly.

AUSTRALIA AND NEW ZEALAND

New Guinea is a big Pacific island with mountains and rain forests.

PAPUA NEW GUINEA

Pacific Ocean

Great Barrier Reef

Coral Sea

**Industrial Area** **Apples** **Citrus Fruit** **Cattle**

**Gold** **Sheep** **Mountains** **Alpine**

**Forest** **Farmland** **Grassland** **Desert**

Queensland

lice prings

uth Australia

Brisbane

New Zealand flag

**New Zealand** is made up of North Island and South Island and several smaller islands. There are lots of mountains and glaciers on South Island. North Island has volcanoes and hot-water springs called geysers.

New Zealand's native Maoris

New South Wales

NEW ZEALAND

Darling River

Sydney

Auckland

North Island

Adelaide

Canberra

Wellington

Murray River

Victoria

Melbourne

South Island

ydney is Australia's rgest city. is is the Sydney pera House.

Bass Strait

Tasman Sea

Tasmania

Hobart

# The Arctic and Antarctica

The Arctic is a cold area of land and sea at the top of the earth.

Antarctica is an area of frozen land at the bottom of the earth.

The top and bottom of the earth are called the Poles.

**Summer** and **winter** each last for six months in polar regions.

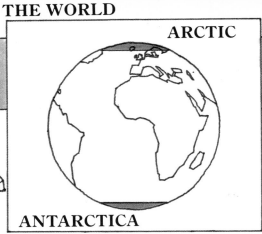
## Polar bears

Many **Arctic animals** only visit in summer, when parts of the land are free of snow. When winter comes, they move farther south or burrow underground. A few creatures, such as polar bears, brave the winter blizzards.

Beaufort Sea

Frozen Arctic Ocean

North Pole

Baffin Bay

Greenland

Barents Sea

ARCTIC

The **Inuit** are a native people of the Arctic. Once they lived in igloos, dome-shaped huts made from ice. They hunted animals and travelled in sleds. Nowadays most of them live in modern settlements and travel on snowmobiles.

**Scientists** visit Antarctica to study the land. They work in **research stations**.

Whale

△ Mountains

☐ Frozen Area

☐ Sea

Mt. Vinson

Greater Antarctica

South Pole

Lesser Antarctica

Mt. Markham

Southern Ocean

ANTARCTICA

Penguin

Seal pup

Hardly any **animals** live in Antarctica because it is too cold and there is almost no food to eat. But **penguins** and other birds live around the coasts. There are also **whales** and **seals** in the sea, where there is plenty of fish for them to eat.